MW01484787

Enhancing U.S. Support
for Peace Operations in Africa

COUNCIL *on*
FOREIGN
RELATIONS

Center for Preventive Action

Council Special Report No. 73
May 2015

Paul D. Williams

Enhancing U.S. Support for Peace Operations in Africa

Contents

Foreword

In the last fifteen years, fifty new peacekeeping operations have been initiated in Africa. Most often led by the United Nations (UN) or the African Union (AU), there are now over one hundred thousand uniformed peacekeepers deployed across the continent serving on a range of missions. The demand on peacekeepers and the countries providing such troops is high due to escalating violence and instability in North Africa and terrorist groups such as al-Shabab. Not surprisingly, the system is under severe pressure, both strategically and financially.

Paul D. Williams, an associate professor in the Elliott School of International Affairs at George Washington University, argues in this Council Special Report that greater U.S. involvement is necessary to enhance the quality and success of peace operations in Africa, which tend to suffer from a lack of trained manpower and inadequate funding. Making matters worse is that these efforts often run up against the reality that personnel are being asked to carry out tasks that go far beyond traditional peacekeeping, leaving troops inadequately prepared to meet the challenges of counterinsurgency, counterterrorism, state-building, and various other duties.

Ultimately, if the UN and AU are going to continue to mount efforts that are, in fact, as much about making as keeping peace, then these organizations will need a deeper pool of countries contributing troops. This will create units with the capability to implement complex, multidimensional mandates with high standards of performance. In order to achieve this, Williams argues that greater U.S. involvement is essential.

The author offers a number of recommendations. He makes the case for a new presidential policy directive on peacekeeping operations, the last one being over twenty years old. Williams suggests, too, that the United States strengthen partnerships with African countries, selecting countries with a proven track record of investing in their own military-education programs and using their own forces to carry out peace-support missions. To bolster multilateral institutions, he suggests that the United States work closely with the UN and AU to develop training programs and performance standards for all peacekeepers. Williams also advocates for the United States increasing personnel commitments to the peacekeeping missions themselves by deploying specialist military contingents. He believes U.S. military expertise in the form of medical, engineering, logistics, and aviation, as well as intelligence, surveillance, and reconnaissance units would be instrumental in increasing the skill and knowledge base of units on the ground. The author understands full well that this proposal raises a host of political and policy questions, and addresses them in the text.

Williams also considers the question of financial resources. Although the United States is already the single largest financial supporter of UN- and African-led peace operations, funding gaps exist for both the UN and the AU. Others in the AU and around the world need to do more, but Williams also calls on Congress to remove its self-imposed funding cap for contributions to such missions.

Enhancing U.S. Support for Peace Operations in Africa offers clear steps that Washington should take to reform the global enterprise of peacekeeping. It provides serious analysis of the current inadequacies of the system and makes recommendations for how to address them. The result is a report that provides a thoughtful assessment of the challenge and a number of recommendations that merit serious consideration and debate.

Richard N. Haass
President
Council on Foreign Relations
May 2015

Acknowledgments

This report has benefitted from the insights and support of numerous people and I am pleased to acknowledge them here. At the Council on Foreign Relations (CFR) I would like to thank Paul B. Stares, Anna Feuer, and Helia Ighani at the Center for Preventive Action (CPA) for initially supporting the idea of writing a report on this topic and for their guidance throughout the subsequent publication process. Stewart M. Patrick and Isabella Bennett in CFR's International Institutions and Global Governance program have my sincere thanks for facilitating travel to the Horn of Africa and U.S. Africa Command, which provided many useful insights. I would also like to thank this report's advisory committee, chaired by Esther Brimmer. Its members offered many useful suggestions on the scope and substance of this report as well as how to frame some of the arguments. CFR President Richard N. Haass and Director of Studies James M. Lindsay also provided useful feedback that helped sharpen the focus and arguments. In Publications, Patricia Dorff and Eli Dvorkin helped produce a more clear and concise report than would have otherwise been the case. Courtney Doggart in Global Communications and Media Relations provided many valuable suggestions on how to market this report.

Outside CFR, thanks are due to numerous officials and personnel within the U.S. government, the African Union, and the United Nations for taking the time to discuss these issues with me. I hope this report can help support the effective peace operations they are working hard to deliver. Other individuals have also influenced my thinking on this topic and offered comments and criticisms of earlier drafts. I am especially grateful to Alex Bellamy, Katharina Coleman, Cedric de Coning, Solomon Dersso, William Durch, Colby Goodman, Richard Gowan, Jordie Hannum, Walter Lotze, and Adam Smith.

This publication was made possible by a grant from Carnegie Corporation of New York. The statements made and views expressed herein are solely my own.

Paul D. Williams

Acronyms

ACIRC	African Capacity for Immediate Response to Crises
ACOTA	Africa Contingency Operations Training and Assistance
ACRI	African Crisis Response Initiative
AFISMA	African-led International Support Mission to Mali
AFRICOM	U.S. Africa Command
AMISOM	African Union Mission in Somalia
APRRP	African Peacekeeping Rapid Response Partnership
AQIM	Al-Qaeda in the Islamic Maghreb
AU	African Union
C-34	UN Special Committee on Peacekeeping Operations
CAR	Central African Republic
CIPA	Contributions for International Peacekeeping Activities
DRC	Democratic Republic of the Congo
EU	European Union
GAO	Government Accountability Office
GPOI	Global Peace Operations Initiative
IED	improvised explosive device
IPPOS	International Police Peacekeeping Operations Support
ISR	intelligence, surveillance, and reconnaissance
MINUSCA	United Nations Multidimensional Integrated Stabilization Mission in the Central African Republic
MINUSMA	United Nations Multidimensional Integrated Stabilization Mission in Mali
MINUSTAH	United Nations Stabilization Mission in Haiti

MISCA	African-led International Support Mission to the Central African Republic
NATO	North Atlantic Treaty Organization
PDD	presidential decision directive
PKO	peacekeeping operations
PPD	presidential policy directive
PSOD	Peace Support Operations Division
REC	regional economic community
SGI	Security Governance Initiative
T/PCC	troop- and/or police-contributing country
UN	United Nations
UNAMID	African Union-United Nations Mission in Darfur
UNMIL	UN Mission in Liberia

Council Special Report

Introduction

Record numbers of peacekeepers are currently deployed in Africa. They undertake critical missions, including stabilizing countries wracked by violence, protecting civilians, facilitating humanitarian assistance, degrading illegal armed groups, running elections, and supporting public security and the rule of law. When deployed in the right circumstances, peace operations have a good track record of facilitating transitions from war to peace as they did in El Salvador, Nicaragua, Namibia, Mozambique, Sierra Leone, Liberia, Cambodia, East Timor, and Bosnia.[1] Evidence is strong that peace operations help protect civilians.[2] Successive U.S. administrations have concluded that such operations serve American interests and national security, are cost-effective, and generate greater legitimacy than U.S. missions carried out alone. In Africa specifically, peace operations promote two of Washington's principal objectives: advancing peace and security and strengthening democratic institutions.[3]

Yet the status quo is untenable, especially given the new multinational task force against Boko Haram in West Africa and perhaps another operation required in Libya following the 2011 U.S.-led intervention. Peace operations on the continent are under severe pressure as a result of multiple failings stemming from peace operations themselves and the international organizations that authorize them, as well as the inadequate efforts of successive U.S. administrations.

First, the current international division of labor is controversial and unsustainable. Countries that mandate United Nations (UN) missions are often different from those that provide the uniformed personnel and contribute major funding. This discrepancy has prompted calls to broaden the base of troop- and/or police-contributing countries (T/PCCs) and raised arguments regarding how the UN Security Council consults those contributors and over operational matters that can hinder mission effectiveness. Second, some missions have struggled to resolve the underlying drivers of instability and violence in their theaters of operation, in large part because they lack real leverage over many conflict parties, especially their host governments. Third, contemporary mandates have often blurred the lines separating peacekeeping, stabilization, counterinsurgency, counterterrorism, atrocity prevention, and state-building. Peacekeepers are rarely trained, equipped, or motivated to deal with such challenges and face a range of daunting operational capability gaps. Finally, the cluster of conflict-management institutions known collectively as the African Peace and Security Architecture remains unfinished.[4] Its institutions are forced to lurch from crisis to crisis and to operate with little indigenous funding. This has undermined the African Union's (AU) credibility as well as its calls for local ownership of Africa's security challenges.

Given the growing interest in fostering a stable and prosperous Africa, the United States should wield its political influence to address these challenges. Yet Washington continues to face internal and external problems related to peace operations. Internally, it lacks a clearly articulated strategic approach to shape policy and to clarify its interagency processes and funding authorities on this issue. The United States has also failed to pay its assessments to UN peacekeeping operations in full and on time. Externally, Washington faces difficult choices about how to identify effective African security partners and strike the appropriate civil-military balance in its support for peace operations. Neither the United States nor the cause of peacekeeping is well served by maintaining one-sided "partnerships" that yield little return on investment.

To better support effective peace operations in Africa, the United States should take the following steps. First, Washington should use selectivity (supporting existing good practices) rather than conditionality (providing assistance on the promise of the recipient reforming its activities in the future) as the principal criterion for choosing bilateral security partners in Africa and devise metrics for evaluating partner performance. Washington should pick and invest in partners that share its conflict-management objectives, design their national security strategies accordingly, and are themselves building locally sustainable peacekeeping institutions. As a litmus test for a more selective U.S. approach, Washington should ask several definitive questions: Did the potential partner invest its resources in building sustainable peacekeeping and other appropriate security institutions? Did it deploy peacekeepers when the opportunity arose? Were those peacekeepers effective on the ground? Does the country help support other U.S. strategic objectives in Africa, including strengthening democracy?

Second, the United States should actively seek opportunities to deploy some of its specialist military contingents to UN peacekeeping operations in combat service and support roles. Deploying these contingents would boost Washington's leadership credentials and leverage at the United Nations, enhance mission effectiveness by closing outstanding capability gaps in the field, and develop a cadre of troops with specialist knowledge of contemporary Africa and contemporary non-NATO multilateral operations and actors that can support and improve future missions on the continent and elsewhere.

Third, the United States should strengthen its support for the crucial multilateral institutions in this area. This will entail increasing its contributions to UN operations; coordinating more closely with the European Union (EU), which has become a major actor in this area since 2003; and supporting the African Union, which now plays a much larger role in addressing the continent's peace and security challenges. The long-term goal of this effort should be to engineer a situation five to ten years from now in which both the UN and the AU can be increasingly selective regarding T/PCCs, drawing on a genuinely global rather than primarily or solely African pool of willing and capable contributors.[5] To strengthen its partnership with the AU, the United States should increase the number of personnel in the U.S. Mission to the AU, establish a predictable funding mechanism to support AU peace operations and headquarters requirements that includes full financial accountability and African contributions, and help the AU develop training and performance standards for its peacekeepers, as well as appropriate metrics for how these standards might be assessed.

Peace Operations in Africa: Patterns and Challenges

Fifty new peace operations have been deployed across Africa since 2000.[6] Several patterns have emerged: the number of peacekeepers, missions, and budgets is constantly on the rise; "partnership peacekeeping" has become the norm on the continent; and African states and the AU play increasingly important roles.

First, the number, size, and cost of peace operations in Africa is growing. By December 2014, approximately 113,000 uniformed peacekeepers were deployed across the continent, more than 11,000 of whom were police officers.[7] The United Nations remains, by far, the single most significant actor, accounting for nearly 82,000 (72.6 percent) of these personnel. African issues also remain the most frequent subject of UN Security Council discussions, and Africa hosts nearly 80 percent of all UN peacekeepers (see figure 1). These figures do not include approximately 15,000 additional civilian personnel in UN peacekeeping operations and more than 600 staff in six UN special political missions currently deployed across Africa.[8] The rising number of personnel involved and the often difficult terrain into which peacekeepers deploy have also significantly increased the cost of these operations.

Second, "partnership peacekeeping" has become the norm. This entails collaboration on active military operations between two or more multilateral institutions or various bilateral actors. Several factors have driven this trend, including widespread recognition that no single actor can cope with Africa's security challenges and that different actors bring comparative advantages. As figure 2 shows, however, most peace operations are authorized or supported by the UN Security Council, demonstrating the enduring significance of the UN brand and legitimacy. In Africa, the central partnerships involve relations among the UN, the AU, the regional economic communities (RECs), the EU, and important bilateral actors—principally France, the United States, and Britain.

FIGURE 1: UNIFORMED UN PEACEKEEPERS DEPLOYED WORLDWIDE AND IN AFRICA, 1990–2014

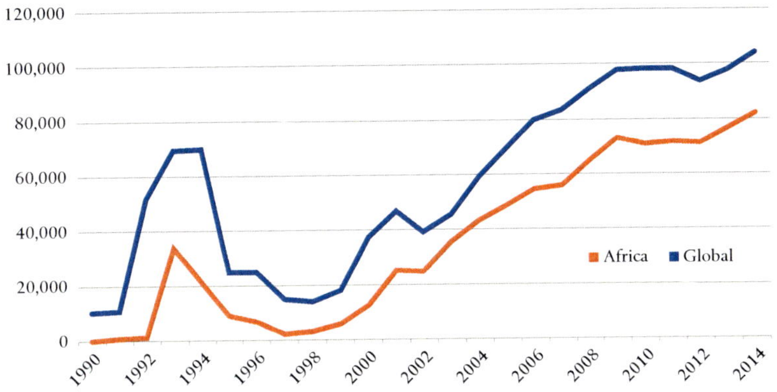

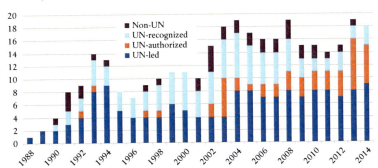

Source: Providing for Peacekeeping Database, November 1990–present, International Peace Institute and George Washington University, http://www.providingforpeacekeeping.org/contributions.

FIGURE 2: NUMBER AND TYPES OF PEACE OPERATIONS IN AFRICA, 1988–2014

Source: Adapted from A. J. Bellamy and P. D. Williams, "Trends in Peace Operations, 1947–2013" in *The Oxford Handbook of United Nations Peacekeeping Operations*, ed. Koops et al. (Oxford: Oxford University Press, forthcoming 2015).

In Africa, partnership peacekeeping has taken several forms. One is sequenced operations, as in Mali, Burundi, and the Central African Republic (CAR), in which responsibility transitions from one set of actors to another, usually from African organizations to the United Nations. In parallel operations, multiple missions coexist simultaneously within the same theater, as in the Democratic Republic of the Congo (DRC), Ivory Coast, and the CAR. The United Nations has also provided a variety of support packages to regional missions, only one of which, in Somalia, was funded from the United Nations' assessed peacekeeping budget. One joint hybrid mission has also been undertaken, between the United Nations and the AU in Darfur, Sudan (UNAMID), though there is little appetite among Western countries to repeat this experiment.

A third pattern has been the consistent increase in African contributions to these peace operations. Moreover, since 2004, the AU has played the central role, authorizing the deployment of more than forty thousand troops, nearly four thousand police, and more than four hundred civilian experts in its four major peace support operations in Darfur, Somalia, Mali, and the CAR (see figure 3). However, this trend has three important caveats. First, these deployments have required significant external assistance. Second, the AU has been unable to deploy adequate numbers of police and other civilian experts on its missions. Third, since 2003, the majority of African peacekeepers have come from roughly one-fifth of the AU's members, particularly Burundi, Egypt, Ethiopia, Ghana, Kenya, Nigeria, Rwanda, Senegal, South Africa, Tanzania, and Uganda.

Peace operations in Africa face a range of strategic and operational challenges that have left many of them struggling to achieve their mandates. These perennial problems highlight the persistent absence of sustained political support as well as the tendency to misapply the peacekeeping tool.

Most important, peace operations are instruments, not strategies. To succeed, they need strong political support and a viable strategy for

FIGURE 3: UNIFORMED PERSONNEL DEPLOYED BY AU MEMBER STATES IN UN AND AU MISSIONS

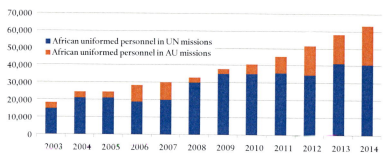

Source: Providing for Peacekeeping Database, November 1990–present, International Peace Institute and George Washington University, http://www.providingforpeacekeeping.org/contributions, and author's calculations.

conflict resolution and reconciliation. Without a viable strategy, peace-keepers may stem some of the worst symptoms of a particular crisis, but they will not resolve the fundamental drivers of violence and instability. This has been a problem for many years in Darfur and the DRC, and more recently in South Sudan, Mali, and the CAR, where peacemakers have failed to resolve conflict and left peacekeepers to pick up the pieces.

To be effective, peace operations need to be part of a broader toolbox of conflict-management instruments for the United Nations, the AU, and other actors to use. For example, peace operations are not always appropriate tools to deliver successful high–level peace negotiations. The United Nations, the AU, and other actors should hence not focus solely on training, equipping, and deploying peacekeepers, but instead develop broader capabilities to track and assess trends in organized violence, carry out preventive diplomacy and mediation through envoys and special political missions, impose targeted sanctions, and promote peacebuilding and reconciliation initiatives.

A second challenge is maintaining good relations with the host state—a crucial factor in the success (or failure) of most peace operations. In Eritrea, Chad, Burundi, and Sudan, the host government has ejected peace operations; in the DRC and South Sudan, the governments have complained bitterly about the peacekeepers but allowed them to stay. This has generated debate over whether peacekeepers should cross the "Darfur line," that is, deploy into theaters where the host regime officially consents to a mission but erects numerous obstacles to hamper its activities.[9] The other challenge related to consent arises when international actors play a role in deciding who counts as the local de jure authorities, as occurred in Ivory Coast after the contested 2010 elections. It is thus crucial that peace operations receive strong and united political support from the UN Security Council or other mandating authority.

Peace operations in Africa also face a range of financial challenges. The United Nations maintains a workable system to pay for its operations, though powerful member states generally try to keep missions as small as possible. In contrast, the AU has a system on paper that has never worked effectively in practice, leaving the AU in a constant search for predictable, sustainable, and flexible funding.[10] The fundamental problem is the lack of major indigenous sources of funding, which has left the AU unable to deploy and sustain peace operations in the field. As a result, African calls for local ownership and leadership are dramatically undermined. This financial reality is reflected in the AU's 2015 budget, in which only $8.7 million (2.3 percent) of its programmatic budget of $379 million is paid for by AU member states: external partners, including the United States, are expected to pay the rest.[11]

Despite the strategic and financial problems, peacekeepers in Africa are routinely mandated to carry out complex, multifaceted, and difficult tasks in highly volatile environments. For example, the most recent UN operation, the Multidimensional Integrated Stabilization Mission in the Central African Republic (MINUSCA), was mandated to implement twenty-seven priority tasks and fourteen additional tasks ranging from protecting civilians "from threat of physical violence" to seizing illicit weapons and promoting "the rapid extension of state authority."[12] Most peacekeepers in Africa work in active war zones where there is no peace to keep—a trend reflected in the now-regular deployment of special forces in several theaters, notably Mali, the DRC, and Somalia. Unsurprisingly, more peacekeepers are dying as a result.[13]

The multifaceted mandates assigned to peace operations have also blurred the lines between activities traditionally kept distinct. Numerous contemporary "peacekeeping" operations in Africa have involved war fighting, stabilization, counterinsurgency, counterterrorism, atrocity prevention, state-building, and regime-consolidation tasks— particularly in the CAR, Mali, the DRC, and Somalia, where the United Nations and the AU have explicitly designated enemy groups. Most of these tasks far outstrip the current principles and guidelines on which UN peacekeeping is based.[14] Consequently, the need to clarify the limits of peace operations and distinguish them from war fighting, counterterrorism, or counterinsurgency is urgent.

Finally, almost every mission in Africa suffers from a variety of operational capability gaps. The standard problems include difficulties with rapid deployment and mission start-up capabilities; logistics supply, which is intensified by operating in environments with little infrastructure, placing a premium on air transport; transportation, including availability of armored vehicles and aviation units; medical and engineering units; intelligence, surveillance, and reconnaissance capabilities; and communications. In addition, suicide bombings and improvised explosive devices (IEDs) pose a range of relatively novel challenges to peacekeepers, especially in Somalia and Mali. Future operations are likely to encounter these threats more frequently.

U.S. Support for Peace Operations in Africa

The U.S. contribution to peace operations in Africa is multidimensional, involving numerous government bodies, most notably the National Security Council staff, the Departments of State and Defense, and the U.S. missions to the United Nations and the AU. It involves relationships with international organizations—the United Nations, AU, RECs, and EU—and major T/PCCs, not all of which are African. Washington's considerable political influence at the United Nations enables it to push for institutional reforms, several of which have come to fruition in recent years. It also remains the largest bilateral donor for peace operations in Africa. The United States has deployed few of its uniformed personnel as peacekeepers in Africa, instead focusing on supporting other actors through various train-and-equip and assistance programs. Over the last year, Washington has provided novel support services for both UN and African missions and has unveiled new initiatives—notably the White House's African Peacekeeping Rapid Response Partnership (APRRP) proposal—and encouraged other countries to boost their own contributions to UN peacekeeping.

POLITICAL INFLUENCE

Both the George W. Bush and Barack Obama administrations have played leading roles in authorizing the expansion of peace operations in Africa through the United States' permanent seat on the UN Security Council. This seat gives the United States significant leverage on many issues, including the ability to veto any envisaged peace operation it does not support. Washington is also uniquely positioned to give strong political support to UN operations, which is particularly important when host governments threaten those missions.

The United States has also used its influence to push for institutional peacekeeping reforms at the United Nations. These include the

New Horizon initiative in 2009, the ongoing development of operational standards for UN peacekeepers, and the Senior Advisory Group process that produced a series of important reforms in late 2012.[15] At the same time, however, and especially since the 2008 financial crisis, Washington has pushed for a financially efficient UN peacekeeping architecture, which has often produced gaps between needs on the ground and the design of force requirements for particular missions. This has encouraged a damaging cycle in which the UN Secretariat fails to present realistic force-requirement options that can deliver on the Security Council's mission mandates. Instead, the design of mission force requirements is more likely to be based on the projected level of available contributions than on an objective assessment of the local needs.[16] This is precisely the wrong way to operate. Influential powers such as the United States should encourage the UN Secretariat to indicate what they need to hear rather than what they want to hear with respect to planning for peace operations.[17]

The expansion of peace operations in Africa and the U.S. push for various institutional reforms at the UN have taken place in the absence of a coherent U.S. strategic policy on peace operations. The last U.S. strategy dedicated to peacekeeping was Presidential Decision Directive 25 (PDD-25), written in 1994 to facilitate the U.S. retreat from UN missions after the debacle in Mogadishu in October 1993. PDD-25 set out restrictive criteria for subsequent U.S. involvement in multilateral peace operations. Since then, references to peacekeeping in relevant U.S. strategic guidance have been infrequent, superficial, and often out of touch with current peacekeeping realities in Africa and elsewhere. This has left the Department of Defense, in particular, with a lack of clarity about the priority that should be accorded to supporting peace operations, especially when specific crises break, as occurred most recently in South Sudan and the CAR.

PERSONNEL DEPLOYMENTS

Since the mid-1990s, the United States has deployed few uniformed personnel in UN peacekeeping operations, most of whom were contracted police officers, military observers, or staff officers rather than troops (see figure 4).[18] Sometimes U.S. staff officers have occupied senior posts in missions, including, recently, the force chief of staff in

FIGURE 4: UNIFORMED U.S. PERSONNEL IN UN PEACEKEEPING OPERATIONS, 1990–2014

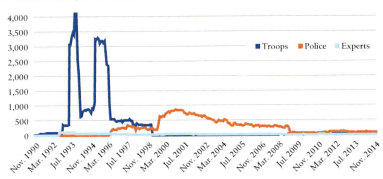

Source: Providing for Peacekeeping Database, November 1990–present, International Peace Institute and George Washington University, http://www.providingforpeacekeeping.org/contributions.

the UN Mission in Liberia (UNMIL). As of January 2015, forty-two U.S. uniformed personnel were deployed in UN peacekeeping operations in Africa.[19] Washington has deployed more troops (special forces and military advisors) on the continent in support of African-led missions to counter the Lord's Resistance Army in central Africa (approximately 280 to 300 personnel) and al-Shabab in Somalia (approximately 120 personnel).[20] In late 2014, a small team of U.S. technical experts deployed to the CAR to oversee the construction of expeditionary bases for MINUSCA's three sector headquarters.[21] Washington's decision in late 2014 to dispatch troops to support the UN and AU anti–Ebola "health-keeping" missions in West Africa was another positive example of a U.S. military deployment.

As a result of such limited deployments and other global strategic priorities, the number of U.S. practitioners with direct experience of UN or AU peace operations is small, and has not expanded significantly since the major U.S. contributions in the Balkans and Somalia during the 1990s.

Whether to deploy more uniformed U.S. personnel to UN operations remains a matter of debate. In April 2013, UN Secretary-General Ban Ki-moon made an unprecedented visit to then U.S. Secretary of Defense Chuck Hagel to request greater U.S. assistance for UN peacekeeping operations. Ban returned the following year, this time focused on obtaining support for the mission in the Central African Republic. Although official support for deploying U.S. infantry battalions in UN operations is minimal, discussions are under way about what roles specialist U.S. military contingents might play in combat service or support roles. These would include predominantly inside-the-wire activities related to medical, engineering, aviation, logistics, as well as intelligence, surveillance, and reconnaissance (ISR) capabilities, which are often in short supply in UN missions.

The United States should look to deploy specialist military contingents as UN "blue helmets" for several reasons. First, deployment would demonstrate Washington's commitment to the idea that UN peacekeeping is a collective global responsibility and an important instrument of international conflict management.

Second, the lack of U.S. personnel in UN peacekeeping missions undermines Washington's attempts to exercise leadership. Leading by example would likely produce better results than asking other states to do something the United States does not do itself. Such deployments would also increase U.S. leverage within other UN forums, such as the Special Committee on Peacekeeping Operations (C-34) and Fourth and Fifth Committees, which are crucial for implementing peacekeeping reforms.[22]

Third, deploying U.S. units, even temporarily, would almost certainly boost mission effectiveness, especially in areas where peacekeepers currently lack necessary enablers, such as aviation, engineering, ISR, or medical capabilities. A fourth argument highlights the importance of skills retention in the U.S. military. Especially after the campaigns in Afghanistan and Iraq, specialist units, such as medics and engineers, will need operational experience to retain core skills. UN peace operations could provide such experience.

U.S. blue helmets would also boost the U.S. military's knowledge of the African continent, the UN peacekeeping system, and fellow contributing countries, including both familiar NATO allies and partners outside NATO, such as China, India, Pakistan, Brazil, and Indonesia. Deploying contingents would thus build a cadre of troops with distinct working knowledge of the UN peacekeeping system the United States seeks to influence.

U.S. involvement would also provide a unique set of operational experiences and exposure to different perspectives. Firsthand knowledge of operational realities in African crisis zones would benefit the U.S. diplomatic corps in Africa, which is retreating behind fortress embassies. Deployment would also support the U.S. Army's new concept of regionally aligned forces, according to which troops are supposed to develop regional familiarity. Eventually, army units will be permanently tasked to support particular geographical areas and will be expected to form relationships with those countries.[23] Deploying in peace operations would help the army achieve this goal.

In contrast, others argue that deploying U.S. blue helmets would be unwise without a larger domestic political consensus that the United States should play this role. Skeptics also suggest that other developed militaries—notably in Europe and Asia—should contribute more peacekeepers because Washington conducts the lion's share of many high–end military tasks related to other global security concerns. Yet Washington should be prepared to deploy its own personnel to advance its interests effectively. Missions such as the recent anti-Ebola operation in West Africa could help build domestic consensus in favor of further deployments. These commitments might also help persuade advanced European and Asian countries to provide more peacekeepers to operations in Africa.

There are also long-standing concerns about placing U.S. troops under UN command and control, which will likely be amplified during a Republican Congress. Such concerns could be overcome, however, by placing U.S. units under UN operational control, or, more accurately, tactical control, while retaining U.S. lines of command.

Skeptics also emphasize other prudential concerns, including the need to avoid theaters where U.S. troops might attract radical extremists and generate counterproductive force-protection risks, or scenarios in which a large U.S. presence would reduce the incentive for local powers to shoulder more responsibility. Such concerns are real but not uniformly present in all missions and should not rule out deployment in principle. It is notable that other Western states face similar challenges yet believe the reasons to deploy outweigh the risks. Military overstretch is another common complaint: even after the drawdown of the Afghanistan and Iraq campaigns, the U.S. military retains a high operational tempo, has little spare capacity, and has endured significant budget cuts since 2009. Deploying U.S. blue helmets would require political leadership to make the case for why they are needed. Ironically, this relative austerity may encourage the military to consider deployments to justify further funding. Finally, the Cold War–era notion that great powers should not participate in peacekeeping efforts persists among skeptics, even though China, Russia, and the United States have all participated in peace operations since the 1990s. Although global reactions to U.S. military contingents in UN operations would undoubtedly be mixed, these operations may also provide opportunities for collaboration with Chinese and Russian partners to enhance peacekeeping missions and bolster military ties.

Other institutional obstacles persist. For one, the current U.S. military profile is not well configured to promote major deployments in UN peace operations. Nevertheless, one potential model is a so-called package contribution, wherein a country deploys enough person-nel—including special forces, ISR capabilities, close air support, and assets for casualty evacuation—to limit its reliance on the UN system and other T/PCCs within the mission. The Netherlands has recently provided such a contribution to the UN operation in Mali. Co-deploy-ment with a partner country is another option, perhaps through shared deployment of Level II medical facilities as pioneered by Norway and Serbia in the UN's mission in Chad in 2009.

Another obstacle is the failure to reward U.S. military personnel, in pay and promotions, for such multilateral deployments, either as con-tingents or individual personnel. These obstacles are more pronounced where the deployment of police officers is concerned because of the lack of a federal police force and the subsequent reliance on private contrac-tors. Although the United States is not well suited to deploying police units to UN missions, it should actively seek opportunities to contribute specialist military contingents in combat service or support roles that align with the UN's operational capability gaps. Offering specialized support is preferable to merely enhancing capacity, which has not been enough to ensure effective peace operations. Deploying a small, select group of specialist contingents would improve the effectiveness of UN operations without adding onerous burdens to current commitments or displacing U.S. military capabilities from future non-UN missions in other parts of the world. The United States can identify generic criteria to guide when, where, and how many personnel should be deployed.

FINANCIAL CONTRIBUTIONS

The United States is the single largest financial supporter of UN and African peace operations in Africa. Washington provides voluntary support to the overall budget of the AU, as well as support to countries involved in peace operations. At the United Nations, the United States is part of a periodic process that currently sets its assessed contributions at 22 percent of the regular budget (which covers special political missions) and 28.4 percent of the peacekeeping budget.[24] Since the United States is a UN member state, these contributions are international treaty obligations. In 1994, however, Congress capped the U.S. contribution, appropriated through its Contributions for International Peacekeeping Activities (CIPA) account, to the UN's assessed peacekeeping budget at 25 percent of the total.[25] Since then, each administration needs to acquire an annual waiver to pay its obligations at the assessed rate above the 25 percent cap, which Congress has refused for the last two years. Part of President Obama's commitment to supporting and reforming UN peacekeeping operations involves increasing U.S. financial support to peace operations in Africa, including efforts to clear the backlog of arrears.

Investing in UN peace operations is generally a good proposition for the United States; these operations are clearly cost-effective when compared with equivalent U.S. deployments and are active in regions where U.S. troops would be unlikely to venture.[26] In 2007, for example, the U.S. Government Accountability Office (GAO) estimated that it would cost the United States roughly eight times as much to conduct a multidimensional peacekeeping operation similar to the UN Stabilization Mission in Haiti (MINUSTAH).[27] Moreover, other countries pay roughly 72 percent of the costs and U.S. businesses are able to recoup a significant portion of those funds by winning contracts to support the UN missions.[28]

The United States also provides financial support to peace operations in Africa through other channels. Two of the most important are the Department of State's Peacekeeping Operations (PKO) account, which supports UN and other peace operations; and the Pentagon's Defense Institution Building, Building Partner Capacity, and International Education and Training programs.[29] The Pentagon's Section 1206 program to train and equip partners in counterterror and stability operations has become particularly important, given the overlap between counterterrorism and peacekeeping activities in some regions, notably Mali and Somalia, and perhaps Nigeria.[30]

In fiscal year (FY) 2013, these financial contributions amounted to approximately $1.7 billion in assessed U.S. contributions to UN peacekeeping in Africa; approximately $100 million to the African-led International Support Mission in Mali (AFISMA); more than $170 million to the African-led International Support Mission in the Central

African Republic (MISCA); more than $500 million to support the
African Union Mission in Somalia (AMISOM); and $35 million to sup-
port operations against the Lord's Resistance Army in central Africa.[31]
In addition, eight African countries received approximately $100 mil-
lion in Section 1206 funding.[32]

ASSISTANCE

U.S. funds have been used to provide T/PCCs and African regional
organizations with logistical and communications support, strategic
airlift, training and equipment (including ammunition in some cases),
ISR, and vehicles. The United States has also supported external forces
to carry out enforcement missions, including France's Operation
Serval in Mali in 2013.

The largest and most enduring mechanisms have been U.S. train-
and-equip programs, notably the Global Peace Operations Initiative
(GPOI) and, on Africa specifically, the African Crisis Response Initiative (ACRI) and its successor, Africa Contingency Operations Training
and Assistance (ACOTA). These programs currently work with twenty
African partner countries and provide training on a wide spectrum of
military tasks (see table 1).[33]

Since 2005, the United States has contributed nearly $1 billion to
support peacekeeping capacities through GPOI, with up to two-thirds
of its expenditure allocated for activities in Africa (see figure 5). Since
2009, the United States has also expended more than $25 million
through the International Police Peacekeeping Operations Support

TABLE 1: U.S. PEACEKEEPING PARTNERS IN AFRICA (AS OF
NOVEMBER 2014)

APRRP Partners	Other ACOTA Partners		Inactive ACOTA Partners
Ethiopia (4)	Benin (24)	Malawi (33)	Botswana (0)
Ghana* (7)	Burkina-Faso (15)	Niger* (17)	Mali* (74)
Rwanda (5)	Burundi (25)	Nigeria* (8)	Mauritania (64)
Senegal (9)	Cameroon (22)	Sierra Leone (70)	Mozambique (0)
Tanzania (11)	Djibouti (62)	South Africa (14)	Namibia (69)
Uganda (85)	Gabon (42)	Togo (19)	
	Kenya (31)	Zambia (65)	

* Also part of the U.S. Security Governance Initiative
(X) Indicates UN contributor ranking as of December 31, 2014.

*FIGURE 5: GPOI ANNUAL BUDGET AND PROPORTION
ALLOCATED TO ACTIVITIES IN AFRICA (U.S. DOLLARS)*

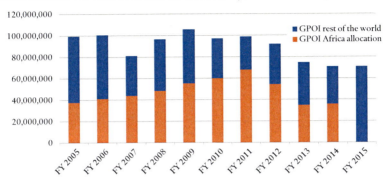

Source: Author's communication with GPOI officials.

*Africa allocations have not yet been made for FY 2015.

(IPPOS) program to train, equip, and support more than 4,500 police from nine partner countries. In addition to training peacekeepers, GPOI has tried to help build the self-sufficiency of partner countries to train their own military peacekeepers by preparing trainers, refurbishing training facilities and infrastructure, and helping partners develop their own peacekeeping instruction programs. During FY 2013, the vast majority of peacekeepers trained under the State Department's PKO account were from Nigeria (5,976), Uganda (5,002), Burundi (4,789), Ghana (2,719), Benin (1,856), Niger (1,403), Sierra Leone (1,278), Togo (1,251), and Somalia (1,060).[34] Since FY 2009, however, GPOI's budget has been cut by approximately one-third.

The U.S. Africa Command (AFRICOM) and the Combined Joint Task Force–Horn of Africa have also provided various forms of assistance to the AU's Peace and Security Department and African T/PCCs. The establishment of the Africa Logistics Council in 2014, in which AFRICOM plays a central coordinating role, is an important development for ensuring that transportation capabilities and systems are put in place to enable peacekeepers to deploy quickly to their respective theaters.

AFRICOM also conducts training exercises focused on headquarters functions and command-and-control arrangements to help African contributors plan, deploy, sustain, and redeploy troops and matériel in peace operations.[35] As the United Nations moves to adopt more operational standards, participation in such exercises is likely to become increasingly significant for African contributors.

The rapid increase in peacekeeping operations in the early 2000s prompted GPOI and ACOTA to adopt a broad rather than deep approach to training African peacekeepers, providing cycles of approximately ten weeks of pre-deployment training across some thirty African countries.[36] These programs improved the ability of those troops to perform relatively basic peacekeeping tasks, but they have struggled in several areas. First, they have difficulty ensuring that the peacekeepers being trained and the equipment being transferred actually deploy to peace operations, which remains the host government's decision. Second, they struggle to devise and implement metrics to measure the performance of these peacekeepers before and after their ACOTA training. Third, the programs have trouble encouraging African contributors to become self-sufficient in this area.

Critics of the U.S. train-and-equip approach have raised several concerns. One is that no objective assessment has been made as to whether this approach works or could instead backfire on U.S. foreign policy goals.[37] Second, increased African experience in peace operations has reduced the need for U.S. instructors on the front lines of training. U.S. experts would be more effective in behind-the-scenes roles, such as helping African officers and noncommissioned officers develop professional military-education programs and institutions.[38] Third, standalone training programs that are not integrated into locally sustainable systems of professional military education will see any benefits erode after about six months. Although training and equipment should help armed forces respond to specific crises, they are at best a short-term band-aid approach to dysfunctional institutions that lack the indigenous resources and personnel required to reproduce such training or maintain equipment. Other critics go further, suggesting that U.S. willingness to continually supply train-and-equip packages to underperforming African states has reduced the incentive for those countries to invest in their own capabilities. A fourth argument suggests that the capabilities that ACOTA can supply—primarily infantry battalions, personal equipment, and vehicles—are not adequate for implementing the mandates and overcoming the challenges of contemporary operations, which require far more kinetic activities, specialist capabilities, and higher numbers of police officers and other civilian experts. At the least, this would suggest a shift in training toward filling crucial UN and AU capability gaps, such as with medical, engineering, ISR, logistics, or special forces units.

NEW INITIATIVES

In 2014, the United States organized two major international summits that launched new initiatives to enhance peace operations in Africa, partly in recognition of this mismatch between supply and demand in contemporary peace operations.

In August 2014, two new initiatives, the African Peacekeeping Rapid Response Partnership (APRRP) and the Security Governance Initiative (SGI), were unveiled at the inaugural U.S.-Africa Leaders Summit.[39] The APRRP's goal is to help the militaries of six African ACOTA partners—Senegal, Ghana, Ethiopia, Rwanda, Tanzania, and Uganda—maintain "forces and equipment ready to rapidly deploy and state their intent to deploy as part of UN or AU missions to respond to emerging crises."[40] Starting in FY 2015, its budget is $110 million per year for three to five years. The rationale behind the APRRP is to fill one of the most commonly cited peacekeeping needs: rapidity of effective deployment in crises when the difference between deploying a force in two weeks or six months could mean tens of thousands of lives. Because only countries with reasonable indigenous capabilities for sustainable expeditionary deployments could hope to deploy within a few weeks, the United States started the APRRP with states that had a proven track record of deployment, a willingness to take on risky mandates, and the institutional capacities to absorb the additional investment. Washington emphasized that the APRRP is not a one-off transaction but rather an ongoing compact in which the African partners will be held accountable for fulfilling their side of the bargain.

The APRRP's unveiling has highlighted some important issues in U.S. policy on peace operations. First, APRRP is another mechanism that involves African states bilaterally without an AU component, though it could support deployments to UN or AU missions.[41] Second, its budget is quite small once apportioned across six countries. Third, as a White House–driven initiative, it remains unclear how far and how fast it will be implemented by other U.S. government bodies, and with what effects. Fourth, questions remain about the choice of initial partner countries, particularly those with poor governance records—notably Ethiopia, Rwanda, and Uganda—whose militaries have abused civilians at home and abroad. Such partnerships risk undermining U.S. credibility on its stated goal of strengthening democratic institutions in Africa.

Fifth, it is not clear that the APRRP partners have much additional deployment capacity (see table 2). Ghana, Rwanda, Senegal, and Uganda already have high proportions of their armies deployed on peace operations, and this excludes Uganda's ongoing operations in South Sudan. Although only 10 percent of Tanzania's army is deployed, the country has only twenty-three thousand personnel, leaving little scope for additional battalion-level deployments. The United States is thus left with Ethiopia, already the world's biggest contributor of uniformed peacekeepers.

In September 2014, the United States organized another summit convened by Vice President Joe Biden that succeeded in generating new peacekeeping commitments from more than thirty countries. Biden said the United States would "review" its contributions to peacekeeping by assessing gaps Washington "is uniquely positioned to fill," sharing the U.S. military's knowledge of "confronting asymmetric threats," and helping the UN "deploy advanced technology."[42] The review of U.S. contributions is ongoing—indeed, there have been internal reviews of one sort or another for the last few years within U.S. government agencies. But the summit did lead to the United Nations' unprecedented purchase of U.S. expeditionary bases for its mission in the CAR, considerable interest from the UN Mine Action Service in whether it could acquire V-shaped anti-mine vehicles for its operations, and the deployment of a U.S. army-assessment team to evaluate how the UN mission in Mali can counter IED threats.[43]

TABLE 2: MILITARY STATISTICS AND PEACE OPERATIONS
DEPLOYMENTS FOR APRRP PARTNERS

	Army	Navy	Air Force	Budget, 2013 Millions of U.S. Dollars	UN PKOs	AU PSOs AMISOM	RCI- LRA	Army Deployed on Peace Ops Percent
Ethiopia	135,000	0	3,000	351	7,827	4,395	0	9.1
Ghana	11,500	2,000	2,000	291	2,969	0	0	25.8
Rwanda	32,000	0	1,000	82	5,667	0	0	17.7
Senegal	11,900	950	750	231	2,836	0	0	23.8
Tanzania	23,000	1,000	3,000	327	2,253	0	0	9.8
Uganda	45,000	0	0	342	30	6,200	2,000	18.3

Source: International Institute for Strategic Studies, The Military Balance 2014 (London: Taylor & Francis, 2014).

Recommendations

In September 2015, the United States will organize a second peacekeeping summit in New York that President Obama will lead to mark the seventieth anniversary of the United Nations. By then, the United Nations will also have released the report of the High-Level Independent Panel on Peace Operations, which could chart the course of UN operations for the foreseeable future. International debates will also intensify over whether European and other contributors to the International Security Assistance Force in Afghanistan will return to UN peacekeeping now that the Afghan campaign is over. In Africa, discussion is likely to focus on whether to deploy new or expanded peace operations to Nigeria, Libya, and perhaps elsewhere.

In this context, Washington should use its political influence to promote a future in which the United Nations and the African Union can draw on a much deeper pool of potential contributing countries with the will and capabilities to implement complex, multidimensional mandates and agree on shared performance standards. The United Nations and the African Union could then become more selective about which peacekeepers and capabilities to deploy on specific missions. With strong and widespread support, developing such a global—rather than solely African—pool of T/PCCs is a realistic goal for the next five years.

The United States can help generate that support by leveraging the premium that many countries still place on working alongside the U.S. military to help persuade other developed militaries to contribute to future peace operations in Africa. The United States should also continue to make innovative contributions to ongoing missions in the interim period, as it has done in Somalia, Mali, the CAR, and elsewhere. To make the most of this opportunity, however, Washington will need to put its own house in order and develop appropriate funding authorities and institutional partnerships to deliver more effective peace operations on the continent. The following steps should be taken:

- *Adopt selectivity rather than conditionality as the principal criterion for choosing U.S. bilateral security partners in Africa, and devise metrics for evaluating partner performance.* The focus of U.S. assistance programs should shift from training and equipping peacekeepers to building sustainable national peacekeeping institutions and expeditionary capabilities. U.S. bilateral partners should therefore be selected on the basis of whether they are investing their own resources in professional military-education programs, designing their forces to carry out expeditionary peace-support tasks, and developing capabilities to fill operational gaps. In line with existing U.S. objectives, preference should also be given to countries that promote good governance and the rule of law at home.

- *Actively seek opportunities to deploy U.S. specialist military contingents to UN peacekeeping operations in combat service and support roles.* The United States should continue its recent innovative activities of deploying specialist capabilities and technical expertise (military, police, and civilian) in support of UN and African missions. Recent initiatives to support UN operations, such as selling expeditionary bases to MINUSCA and conducting assessments of the asymmetric threats facing MINUSMA, are important and should be replicated where appropriate. But the United States should also seek opportunities to deploy specialist military capabilities and contingents in combat service and support roles in UN peacekeeping operations in Africa. Priority capabilities in Africa would include medical, engineering, logistics, aviation, and ISR units. Co-deployment of, for instance, a Level II hospital unit with a partner country is one model to consider. Alternatively, the United States might look to deploy a package contribution of capabilities and assets, as the Netherlands has committed to MINUSMA. Deploying U.S. blue helmets would buy significant political goodwill, demonstrate U.S. commitment to the idea that UN peacekeeping is a collective global enterprise, encourage more developed militaries to participate in peacekeeping, and strengthen the skills and knowledge base of the units concerned.

- *Produce a presidential policy directive (PPD) on peace operations.* Without a clear intellectual foundation, U.S. policy on peace operations will continue to lurch ad hoc from crisis to crisis. The Obama administration arrived in office touting the need to strengthen UN peacekeeping as a cost-effective way to deliver "important results by protecting civilians, helping to rebuild security, and advancing peace around the world."[44] Six years on, the administration should state its policy and strategic approach to peace operations in a single document. This directive should outline the strategic opportunity and need related to peace operations; how the United States can contribute to this issue, including via military, police, and civilian components; and how to work with relevant partners. A PPD would also enable the Pentagon to produce its own strategic guidance on the priority military tasks related to peace operations. Regarding Africa specifically, the PPD should clarify how Washington will enhance its involvement with both the United Nations and the AU. This would necessitate expanding the U.S.-AU mission as the main point of interface, in part to help offset the domination of U.S. bilateral relationships on these issues.

- *Increase investment in U.S. multilateral coordination with both the United Nations and the African Union, to include increasing the number of personnel at the U.S. Mission to the AU.* Washington should increase the number of personnel (civilian and military) directly involved with these crucial multilateral institutions. The U.S. armed forces and Department of Defense in particular should develop a cadre of personnel with direct experience of working in and with the UN and the AU. At the United Nations, the United States should focus on seeking more staff-officer positions within UN peacekeeping operations while deploying specialist military contingents. Ideally, the United States should deploy one to two staff officers or military experts in all sixteen UN peacekeeping operations. The United States could also further leverage its position by adding approximately five additional personnel to work within the UN Military Staff Committee to coordinate and channel military advice to the Security Council. At the AU, the United States should enlarge its mission by adding more Foreign Service officers and military advisors. One model might be the U.S. Mission to the Organization for Security and Cooperation in Europe, which has more than thirty staff members, whereas the U.S. Mission to the AU has fewer than ten. U.S. technical expertise would be particularly useful in helping the AU assess, plan, manage, and evaluate missions and in developing the AU's institutional knowledge by sharing U.S. lessons learned related to developing rapid-reaction forces, including from the stabilization campaigns in Iraq and Afghanistan. Developing a Peace Support Operations Division

(PSOD) intelligence group should also be pursued, which would require a classified military intelligence–sharing agreement.

- *Establish a predictable funding mechanism to support AU peace operations and headquarters requirements that includes full financial accountability and African contributions.* The United States should establish a fund to support the AU directly rather than rely almost entirely on bilateral assistance to African T/PCCs. This fund should be contingent on some level of matching funds from the AU member states to demonstrate their commitment to the enterprise (perhaps a dollar from the AU for every two or three dollars in U.S. contributions). One possible model is the EU's African Peace Facility, which supports the EU's joint strategy with the African Union with a budget of approximately 750 million euros for 2014 through 2016.[45] Such financial support focuses on supporting the headquarters requirements needed to manage African missions, including staffing the AU's PSOD, which is chronically short staffed.[46] Washington should also support the 2008 Prodi Panel's recommendation to use the UN's assessed peacekeeping budget on a case-by-case basis to support African missions the UN Security Council has authorized.[47] The United States should push for the inclusion of a mechanism to ensure oversight of the disbursement of such funds.

- *Assist the UN and the AU in developing training and performance standards for their peacekeepers and appropriate assessment metrics.* U.S. support for the new UN military–unit manuals has been an important first step toward defining and disseminating shared expectations about performance standards for UN peacekeepers. The United States should ensure the process continues with the development of specific training standards and methodologies for assessing peacekeeper performance in the field. The AU should also be encouraged to adopt appropriate standards for its peace support operations.

- *Remove the funding cap on U.S. financial contributions to UN peace operations and pay U.S. assessments in full and on time.* Unfortunately, the U.S. Congress has long ignored calls for the United States to pay its UN peacekeeping assessments in full and on time. Moreover, progress on this issue remains unlikely, at least in the short term. Yet UN peace operations directly and cost-effectively support U.S. national security interests. Consequently, the congressional funding cap on U.S. financial contributions to UN peacekeeping operations should be removed and any incurred arrears paid off. The cap is shortsighted, counterproductive, and breaches U.S. obligations under the UN Charter. The persistent failure by Congress to cover the full assessment rate affects the ability of missions to deliver their mandates on the ground and creates tensions between the United States and major UN T/PCCs whose reimbursements are delayed.

Conclusion

The United Nations and the African Union can conduct and ensure effective peace operations only if they are tied to a comprehensive political strategy of conflict resolution. The effectiveness of these operations depends on the ability of the authorizing bodies to select appropriate contributions from a broad pool of countries able to field well-trained, equipped, and committed peacekeepers, soldiers, police, and civilians. This, in turn, is more likely if peace operations are viewed as a collective global responsibility. The United States should therefore encourage other developed states to invest more personnel and resources in peace operations. Washington's leadership would be enhanced by deploying its own specialist contingents and capabilities within UN missions. The administration should make the case for such deployments as part of a U.S. strategy to support effective, responsive, and multilateral peace operations and it should strengthen its cooperation with the AU and coordination with the EU to help implement that vision.

Endnotes

1. See, for example, V. P. Fortna, *Does Peacekeeping Work? Shaping Belligerents' Choices After Civil War* (Princeton, NJ: Princeton University Press, 2008); A. Heoffler, "Can International Interventions Secure the Peace?" *Area Studies Review* 17, no. 1 (2014): 75–94; and *Human Security Report 2013: The Decline in Global Violence: Evidence, Explanation, and Contestation* (Vancouver: Human Security Press, 2013).
2. L. Hultman, J. Kathman, and M. Shannon, "United Nations Peacekeeping and Civilian Protection in Civil War," *American Journal of Political Science* 57, no. 4 (2013): 875–91.
3. The other two principal objectives are to spur economic growth, trade, and investment, and promote opportunity and development. "U.S. Strategy Toward Sub-Saharan Africa," White House, June 14, 2012, https://www.whitehouse.gov/sites/default/files/rss_viewer/national_security_strategy.pdf. See also "National Security Strategy," White House, May 2010, pp. 44–48, http://www.state.gov/documents/organization/209377.pdf.
4. The principal APSA institutions are the Peace and Security Council, the African Standby Force, the Continental Early Warning System, the Peace Fund, the Panel of the Wise, and the relevant Regional Economic Communities and regional mechanisms.
5. On which, see Adam C. Smith and Arthur Boutellis, "Rethinking Force Generation: Filling Capability Gaps in UN Peacekeeping," International Peace Institute, May 2013.
6. For details to mid-2013, see Paul D. Williams, "Peace Operations in Africa: Lessons Learned Since 2000," Africa Security Brief no. 25, National Defense University, July 2013. I define peace operations broadly as the expeditionary use of uniformed personnel (troops, military observers/experts, and police), with or without a UN mandate, but with an explicit mandate to: assist in the prevention of armed conflict by supporting a peace process; serve as an instrument to observe or assist in the implementation of ceasefires or peace agreements; or enforce ceasefires, peace agreements, or the will of the UN Security Council in order to build stable peace. This excludes what the UN calls special political missions.
7. A total of 81,998 troops are deployed in nine UN-led missions: 22,126 in AMISOM, 5,000 in RCI-LRA, 629 in ECOMIB, 1,000 in EUFOR RCA, 2,000 French troops in Operation Sangaris (Central African Republic), and 450 in Operation Licorne (Ivory Coast). These figures do not include various ongoing training and security sector reform missions on the continent.
8. The countries are Burundi, Guinea-Bissau, Central Africa, West Africa, Libya, and Somalia.
9. Bruce Jones, Richard Gowan, and Jake Sherman, "Building on Brahimi: Peacekeeping in an Era of Strategic Uncertainty," New York University Center on International Cooperation, April 2009, p. 12.
10. The Protocol Relating to the Establishment of the Peace and Security Council of the African Union (2002) stipulates a funding system whereby member states contributing

contingents bear the cost of their participation during the first three months and the AU commits to reimburse those states within a maximum period of six months and then proceed to finance the operation. It was not until January 2013 that the AU, for the first time, decided to cover part of the cost of one of its peace support operations (the African stabilization mission in Mali, AFISMA) from assessed contributions of AU member states.

11. African Union, Executive Council Twenty-Fifth Ordinary Session, June 20–24, 2014, Doc. EX.CL/828(XXV), p. 1, http://www.au.int/en/sites/default/files/EX%20CL%20 Dec%20813%20-%20850%20%28XXV%29%20_E.pdf.

12. UN Security Council, Resolution 2149, April 10, 2014.

13. More than one hundred UN peacekeepers have died in all but one of the last twelve years. Most UN fatalities remain due to illness, especially in Africa's malarial zones, rather than malicious attacks, which have remained relatively steady over the last decade. The AU, however, has suffered the majority of its fatalities during combat in its Somalia operation.

14. See *United Nations Peacekeeping Operations: Principles and Guidelines* (New York: UN Department of Peacekeeping Operations and Department of Field Support, 2008).

15. The UN's emerging standards are based on a dozen UN military–unit manuals, the first of which, in August 2012, focused on UN infantry battalions. The manuals are an important step toward developing common UN training standards across the spectrum of military peacekeeping activities and should facilitate greater interoperability as well as design a baseline for evaluating unit performance. Among the most significant Senior Advisory Group recommendations were longer troop rotations to preserve institutional memory, reductions in reimbursement to countries whose peacekeepers deploy without the necessary equipment to perform their duties, financial premiums for countries providing critical enabling capabilities (such as engineering or aviation units), and provision of danger pay to troops who comport themselves well in areas of elevated risk.

16. See Smith and Boutellis, "Rethinking Force Generation," p. 9; and "Letter dated 2 January 2015 from the Secretary-General addressed to the President of the Security Council" (UN Doc. S/2015/3, January 5, 2015), p. 8.

17. A point made by the Brahimi Panel in 2000. See "The Report of the Panel on United Nations Peace Operations" (UN Doc. A/55/305-S/2000/809, August 17, 2000).

18. For UN peacekeeping operations, old legislation still constrains the extent and nature of U.S. participation, including a baseline limit of one thousand U.S. troops at any one time. The United States is also limited to providing free of charge to the UN no more than $3 million worth of items or services—such as supplies, transportation assistance, or equipment—to each operation per year. United Nations Participation Act of 1945, Pub. L. No. 79-264, sec. 10, December 20, 1945.

19. Twenty-seven troops, eleven police, and four experts in MINUSCA (3), MINUSMA (10), MONUSCO (3), UNMIL (10), and UNMISS (16).

20. "Letter from the President—IDLs—War Powers Resolution," White House, March 25, 2014, http://www.whitehouse.gov/the-press-office/2014/03/25/letter-president-idls-war-powers-resolution; and Phil Stewart, "U.S. discloses secret Somalia military presence, up to 120 troops," *Reuters*, July 2, 2014.

21. After the UN purchased these bases from the United States, the technical team utilized local labor from the UN mission to prepare and erect the bases. Each sector headquarters base has capacity to house three hundred personnel. This is the first time the United States has provided such support to a UN peacekeeping operation.

22. It might also facilitate more U.S. military officers gaining experience of working within the UN, specifically the Office of Military Affairs within the Department of

Peacekeeping Operations (DPKO), where Washington currently retains just one seconded officer.

23. Drew Brooks, "Army Leaders Discuss Benefits of a Regionally Aligned Force," *Fayetteville Observer*, October 15, 2014.

24. These funds are drawn from three accounts at the U.S. Department of State: the Contributions to International Organizations account, which covers the regular UN budget; Contributions to International Peacekeeping Activities, which supports U.S.-assessed contributions to UN peacekeeping operations; and the Peacekeeping Response Mechanism (as part of the President's Overseas Contingency Operations fund), which in FY2015 will also cover U.S. financial obligations for MINUSCA because the mission was authorized after the Obama administration submitted its FY 2015 budget. Because the U.S. budget is set in advance of the fiscal year, it is unable to foresee new developments.

25. Pub. L. No. 103-236, 108 STAT. 447, April 30, 1994.

26. Calculating precise figures for AU and REC operations is considerably more difficult because of the ad hoc funding models used thus far and because they have used variable rates of monthly allowances for their peacekeepers.

27. Statement of Joseph A. Christoff, "Peacekeeping: Observations on Costs, Strengths, and Limitations of U.S. and UN Operations," testimony before the Subcommittee on International Organizations, Human Rights, and Oversight, Committee on Foreign Affairs, U.S. House of Representatives, June 13, 2007, http://www.gao.gov/products/GAO-07-998T.

28. Although this varies annually, U.S. firms have received the largest slice of UN procurement contracts each year since 2005. In 2013, for example, U.S. firms procured more than $750 million in UN services, more than double the nearest competitors (United Arab Emirates and Russia). See UN Procurement Division, http://www.un.org/Depts/ptd/statistics/2013.

29. See Defense Security Cooperation Agency, http://www.dsca.mil/programs.

30. Section 1206 is a temporary authority granted to the U.S. Department of Defense in 2006 to build partnership capacity in the realm of counterterrorist operations or to participate in or support military and stability operations involving the U.S. armed forces. It is slated to become a permanent authority for the Pentagon under the 2016 National Defense Authorization Act. Section 1206 funding to AMISOM was the first time the United States had supported T/PCCs to address a terror threat beyond its borders, in this case from al-Shabab. See "Section 1206 Train and Equip," Defense Security Cooperation Agency, http://www.dsca.mil/programs/section-1206-train-and-equip.

31. "U.S. Support for Peacekeeping in Africa," White House, August 6, 2014; and Alexis Arieff and Lauren Ploch, "The Lord's Resistance Army: The U.S. Response," Congressional Research Service report no. R42094, May 15, 2014, p. 13.

32. Burkina Faso, Burundi, Chad, Kenya, Libya, Mauritania, Niger, and Uganda. Nina M. Serafino, "Security Assistance Reform: 'Section 1206' Background and Issues for Congress," Congressional Research Service report no. RS22855, December 8, 2014, p. 7.

33. For an overview, see "Global Peace Operations Initiative (GPOI)," U.S. Department of State, http://www.state.gov/r/pa/prs/ps/2014/09/232265.htm. Since 2008, any U.S. military training of foreign security forces needs to conform with the terms of the Leahy Law, which prohibits military assistance to foreign units that have committed a "gross violation of human rights." If the Leahy vetting process finds evidence that an individual or unit has committed such violations, U.S. assistance should be withheld and the secretary of state should "assist the foreign government in taking effective measures to bring the responsible members of the security forces to justice." On

occasion, the AU has raised concerns about cases where units accepted for its operations have subsequently failed Leahy vetting.

34. See *Foreign Military Training, Joint Report to Congress Fiscal Years 2013 and 2014*, 2 vols. (U.S. Department of State and U.S. Department of Defense, March 26, 2014), http://www.state.gov/documents/organization/230192.pdf.

35. AFRICOM's Accord series of exercises are aligned with the needs of specific peace operations. Others involving special forces also include thinking about how they could contribute to UN and AU peace operations.

36. Private contractors rather than regular U.S. military personnel delivered much of this training.

37. Gordon Adams, "Ties That Bind," *Foreign Policy*, October 1, 2014.

38. Daniel Hampton, "Creating Sustainable Peacekeeping Capability in Africa," Africa Security Brief no. 27, National Defense University, April 2014.

39. The SGI is a new presidential initiative focused on enhancing security sector assistance in six African countries: Ghana, Kenya, Mali, Niger, Nigeria, and Tunisia. Few details are currently available about its implementation.

40. "Fact Sheet: U.S. Support for Peacekeeping in Africa," White House, August 6, 2014, https://www.whitehouse.gov/the-press-office/2014/08/06/fact-sheet-us-support-peacekeeping-africa.

41. In Africa, the APRRP generated debate over whether it signaled that U.S. support would henceforth focus on the new African Capacity for Immediate Response to Crises (ACIRC) in favor of attempts to operationalize the older African Standby Force concept.

42. Joseph R. Biden, "Opening Remarks by the Vice President at the UN Summit for Peacekeeping Operations," speech delivered at the United Nations, September 26, 2014, http://www.whitehouse.gov/the-press-office/2014/09/26/opening-remarks-vice-president-un-summit-peacekeeping-operations.

43. The latter was facilitated by Section 1206 funding because of the threat posed by al-Qaeda in the Islamic Maghreb (AQIM) in Mali.

44. Barack Obama, "Strengthening UN Peacekeeping to Meet 21st Century Challenges," speech delivered at the United Nations, September 23, 2009, http://usun.state.gov/briefing/statements/2009/september/129601.htm.

45. See "African Peace Facility," European Commission, http://ec.europa.eu/europeaid/node/1519_en; and "Joint Africa-EU Strategy," European Commission, https://ec.europa.eu/europeaid/regions/africa/continental-cooperation/joint-africa-eu-strategy_en.

46. The AU PSOD operates with approximately fifty personnel, only two of which are permanent posts funded by the AU Commission. In 2008, a UN consultancy team concluded that PSOD required two hundred personnel to implement its mandate effectively.

47. "Report of the African Union–United Nations Panel on Modalities for Support to African Union Peacekeeping Operations," UN Doc. A/63/666–S/2008/813, December 31, 2008.

About the Author

Paul D. Williams is an associate professor in the Elliott School of International Affairs at the George Washington University. Williams is also a nonresident senior advisor at the International Peace Institute in New York, where he helps manage the Providing for Peacekeeping Project, an independent research project that analyzes how to develop more effective UN peacekeeping operations. He previously taught at the Universities of Aberystwyth, Birmingham, and Warwick in the United Kingdom and has been a visiting scholar at Georgetown University and the University of Queensland, Australia, as well as a visiting professor at the Institute for Peace and Security Studies at Addis Ababa University, Ethiopia. Williams currently serves on the editorial boards of several scholarly journals: *African Affairs*, *International Peacekeeping*, *Global Governance*, and *Global Responsibility to Protect*. His books include *Understanding Peacekeeping*, *War and Conflict in Africa*, and *Providing Peacekeepers: The Politics, Challenges, and Future of UN Peacekeeping Contributions*.

Advisory Committee for *Enhancing U.S. Support for Peace Operations in Africa*

Catherine A. Bertini
Syracuse University

Esther D. Brimmer
*Elliott School of International Affairs,
George Washington University*

John Campbell, *ex officio*
Council on Foreign Relations

Johnnie Carson
U.S. Institute of Peace

Jack Christofides
United Nations

Joseph J. Collins
National Defense University

Chester A. Crocker
*Edmund A. Walsh School of Foreign Service,
Georgetown University*

Alison Giffen
Stimson Center

Daniel Hampton, USA (Ret.)
National Defense University

Lise M. Howard
Georgetown University

Princeton N. Lyman
Princeton Lyman and Associates

James A. Schear
*Woodrow Wilson International Center
for Scholars*

Paul B. Stares, *ex officio*
Council on Foreign Relations

William E. Ward
U.S. Army (Ret.)

Center for Preventive Action
Advisory Committee

Mission Statement of the Center for Preventive Action

The Center for Preventive Action (CPA) seeks to help prevent, defuse, or resolve deadly conflicts around the world and to expand the body of knowledge on conflict prevention. It does so by creating a forum in which representatives of governments, international organizations, nongovernmental organizations, corporations, and civil society can gather to develop operational and timely strategies for promoting peace in specific conflict situations. The Center focuses on conflicts in countries or regions that affect U.S. interests, but may be otherwise overlooked; where prevention appears possible; and when the resources of the Council on Foreign Relations can make a difference. The Center does this by

- Issuing Council Special Reports to evaluate and respond rapidly to developing conflict situations and formulate timely, concrete policy recommendations that the U.S. government and international and local actors can use to limit the potential for deadly violence.

- Engaging the U.S. government and news media in conflict prevention efforts. CPA staff members meet with administration officials and members of Congress to brief on CPA findings and recommendations; facilitate contacts between U.S. officials and important local and external actors; and raise awareness among journalists of potential flashpoints around the globe.

- Building networks with international organizations and institutions to complement and leverage the Council's established influence in the U.S. policy arena and increase the impact of CPA recommendations.

- Providing a source of expertise on conflict prevention to include research, case studies, and lessons learned from past conflicts that policymakers and private citizens can use to prevent or mitigate future deadly conflicts.

Council Special Reports

Published by the Council on Foreign Relations

Revising U.S. Grand Strategy Toward China
Robert D. Blackwill and Ashley J. Tellis; CSR No. 72, March 2015

Strategic Stability in the Second Nuclear Age
Gregory D. Koblentz; CSR No. 71, November 2014

U.S. Policy to Counter Nigeria's Boko Haram
John Campbell; CSR No. 70, November 2014
A Center for Preventive Action Report

Limiting Armed Drone Proliferation
Micah Zenko and Sarah Kreps; CSR No. 69, June 2014
A Center for Preventive Action Report

Reorienting U.S. Pakistan Strategy: From Af-Pak to Asia
Daniel S. Markey; CSR No. 68, January 2014

Afghanistan After the Drawdown
Seth G. Jones and Keith Crane; CSR No. 67, November 2013
A Center for Preventive Action Report

The Future of U.S. Special Operations Forces
Linda Robinson; CSR No. 66, April 2013

Reforming U.S. Drone Strike Policies
Micah Zenko; CSR No. 65, January 2013
A Center for Preventive Action Report

Countering Criminal Violence in Central America
Michael Shifter; CSR No. 64, April 2012
A Center for Preventive Action Report

Saudi Arabia in the New Middle East
F. Gregory Gause III; CSR No. 63, December 2011
A Center for Preventive Action Report

Partners in Preventive Action: The United States and International Institutions
Paul B. Stares and Micah Zenko; CSR No. 62, September 2011
A Center for Preventive Action Report

Justice Beyond The Hague: Supporting the Prosecution of International Crimes in National Courts
David A. Kaye; CSR No. 61, June 2011

The Drug War in Mexico: Confronting a Shared Threat
David A. Shirk; CSR No. 60, March 2011
A Center for Preventive Action Report

UN Security Council Enlargement and U.S. Interests
Kara C. McDonald and Stewart M. Patrick; CSR No. 59, December 2010
An International Institutions and Global Governance Program Report

Congress and National Security
Kay King; CSR No. 58, November 2010

Toward Deeper Reductions in U.S. and Russian Nuclear Weapons
Micah Zenko; CSR No. 57, November 2010
A Center for Preventive Action Report

Internet Governance in an Age of Cyber Insecurity
Robert K. Knake; CSR No. 56, September 2010
An International Institutions and Global Governance Program Report

From Rome to Kampala: The U.S. Approach to the 2010 International Criminal Court Review Conference
Vijay Padmanabhan; CSR No. 55, April 2010

Strengthening the Nuclear Nonproliferation Regime
Paul Lettow; CSR No. 54, April 2010
An International Institutions and Global Governance Program Report

The Russian Economic Crisis
Jeffrey Mankoff; CSR No. 53, April 2010

Somalia: A New Approach
Bronwyn E. Bruton; CSR No. 52, March 2010
A Center for Preventive Action Report

The Future of NATO
James M. Goldgeier; CSR No. 51, February 2010
An International Institutions and Global Governance Program Report

The United States in the New Asia
Evan A. Feigenbaum and Robert A. Manning; CSR No. 50, November 2009
An International Institutions and Global Governance Program Report

Intervention to Stop Genocide and Mass Atrocities: International Norms and U.S. Policy
Matthew C. Waxman; CSR No. 49, October 2009
An International Institutions and Global Governance Program Report

Enhancing U.S. Preventive Action
Paul B. Stares and Micah Zenko; CSR No. 48, October 2009
A Center for Preventive Action Report

The Canadian Oil Sands: Energy Security vs. Climate Change
Michael A. Levi; CSR No. 47, May 2009
A Maurice R. Greenberg Center for Geoeconomic Studies Report

The National Interest and the Law of the Sea
Scott G. Borgerson; CSR No. 46, May 2009

Lessons of the Financial Crisis
Benn Steil; CSR No. 45, March 2009
A Maurice R. Greenberg Center for Geoeconomic Studies Report

Global Imbalances and the Financial Crisis
Steven Dunaway; CSR No. 44, March 2009
A Maurice R. Greenberg Center for Geoeconomic Studies Report

Eurasian Energy Security
Jeffrey Mankoff; CSR No. 43, February 2009

Preparing for Sudden Change in North Korea
Paul B. Stares and Joel S. Wit; CSR No. 42, January 2009
A Center for Preventive Action Report

Averting Crisis in Ukraine
Steven Pifer; CSR No. 41, January 2009
A Center for Preventive Action Report

Congo: Securing Peace, Sustaining Progress
Anthony W. Gambino; CSR No. 40, October 2008
A Center for Preventive Action Report

Deterring State Sponsorship of Nuclear Terrorism
Michael A. Levi; CSR No. 39, September 2008

China, Space Weapons, and U.S. Security
Bruce W. MacDonald; CSR No. 38, September 2008

Sovereign Wealth and Sovereign Power: The Strategic Consequences of American Indebtedness
Brad W. Setser; CSR No. 37, September 2008
A Maurice R. Greenberg Center for Geoeconomic Studies Report

Securing Pakistan's Tribal Belt
Daniel S. Markey; CSR No. 36, July 2008 (web-only release) and August 2008
A Center for Preventive Action Report

Avoiding Transfers to Torture
Ashley S. Deeks; CSR No. 35, June 2008

Global FDI Policy: Correcting a Protectionist Drift
David M. Marchick and Matthew J. Slaughter; CSR No. 34, June 2008
A Maurice R. Greenberg Center for Geoeconomic Studies Report

Dealing with Damascus: Seeking a Greater Return on U.S.-Syria Relations
Mona Yacoubian and Scott Lasensky; CSR No. 33, June 2008
A Center for Preventive Action Report

Climate Change and National Security: An Agenda for Action
Joshua W. Busby; CSR No. 32, November 2007
A Maurice R. Greenberg Center for Geoeconomic Studies Report

Planning for Post-Mugabe Zimbabwe
Michelle D. Gavin; CSR No. 31, October 2007
A Center for Preventive Action Report

The Case for Wage Insurance
Robert J. LaLonde; CSR No. 30, September 2007
A Maurice R. Greenberg Center for Geoeconomic Studies Report

Reform of the International Monetary Fund
Peter B. Kenen; CSR No. 29, May 2007
A Maurice R. Greenberg Center for Geoeconomic Studies Report

Nuclear Energy: Balancing Benefits and Risks
Charles D. Ferguson; CSR No. 28, April 2007

Nigeria: Elections and Continuing Challenges
Robert I. Rotberg; CSR No. 27, April 2007
A Center for Preventive Action Report

The Economic Logic of Illegal Immigration
Gordon H. Hanson; CSR No. 26, April 2007
A Maurice R. Greenberg Center for Geoeconomic Studies Report

The United States and the WTO Dispute Settlement System
Robert Z. Lawrence; CSR No. 25, March 2007
A Maurice R. Greenberg Center for Geoeconomic Studies Report

Bolivia on the Brink
Eduardo A. Gamarra; CSR No. 24, February 2007
A Center for Preventive Action Report

After the Surge: The Case for U.S. Military Disengagement From Iraq
Steven N. Simon; CSR No. 23, February 2007

Darfur and Beyond: What Is Needed to Prevent Mass Atrocities
Lee Feinstein; CSR No. 22, January 2007

Avoiding Conflict in the Horn of Africa: U.S. Policy Toward Ethiopia and Eritrea
Terrence Lyons; CSR No. 21, December 2006
A Center for Preventive Action Report

Living with Hugo: U.S. Policy Toward Hugo Chávez's Venezuela
Richard Lapper; CSR No. 20, November 2006
A Center for Preventive Action Report

Reforming U.S. Patent Policy: Getting the Incentives Right
Keith E. Maskus; CSR No. 19, November 2006
A Maurice R. Greenberg Center for Geoeconomic Studies Report

Foreign Investment and National Security: Getting the Balance Right
Alan P. Larson and David M. Marchick; CSR No. 18, July 2006
A Maurice R. Greenberg Center for Geoeconomic Studies Report

Challenges for a Postelection Mexico: Issues for U.S. Policy
Pamela K. Starr; CSR No. 17, June 2006 (web-only release) and November 2006

U.S.-India Nuclear Cooperation: A Strategy for Moving Forward
Michael A. Levi and Charles D. Ferguson; CSR No. 16, June 2006

Generating Momentum for a New Era in U.S.-Turkey Relations
Steven A. Cook and Elizabeth Sherwood-Randall; CSR No. 15, June 2006

Peace in Papua: Widening a Window of Opportunity
Blair A. King; CSR No. 14, March 2006
A Center for Preventive Action Report

Neglected Defense: Mobilizing the Private Sector to Support Homeland Security
Stephen E. Flynn and Daniel B. Prieto; CSR No. 13, March 2006

Afghanistan's Uncertain Transition From Turmoil to Normalcy
Barnett R. Rubin; CSR No. 12, March 2006
A Center for Preventive Action Report

Preventing Catastrophic Nuclear Terrorism
Charles D. Ferguson; CSR No. 11, March 2006

Getting Serious About the Twin Deficits
Menzie D. Chinn; CSR No. 10, September 2005
A Maurice R. Greenberg Center for Geoeconomic Studies Report

Both Sides of the Aisle: A Call for Bipartisan Foreign Policy
Nancy E. Roman; CSR No. 9, September 2005

Forgotten Intervention? What the United States Needs to Do in the Western Balkans
Amelia Branczik and William L. Nash; CSR No. 8, June 2005
A Center for Preventive Action Report

A New Beginning: Strategies for a More Fruitful Dialogue with the Muslim World
Craig Charney and Nicole Yakatan; CSR No. 7, May 2005

Power-Sharing in Iraq
David L. Phillips; CSR No. 6, April 2005
A Center for Preventive Action Report

Giving Meaning to "Never Again": Seeking an Effective Response to the Crisis in Darfur and Beyond
Cheryl O. Igiri and Princeton N. Lyman; CSR No. 5, September 2004

Freedom, Prosperity, and Security: The G8 Partnership with Africa: Sea Island 2004 and Beyond
J. Brian Atwood, Robert S. Browne, and Princeton N. Lyman; CSR No. 4, May 2004

Addressing the HIV/AIDS Pandemic: A U.S. Global AIDS Strategy for the Long Term
Daniel M. Fox and Princeton N. Lyman; CSR No. 3, May 2004
Cosponsored with the Milbank Memorial Fund

Challenges for a Post-Election Philippines
Catharin E. Dalpino; CSR No. 2, May 2004
A Center for Preventive Action Report

Stability, Security, and Sovereignty in the Republic of Georgia
David L. Phillips; CSR No. 1, January 2004
A Center for Preventive Action Report

Note: Council Special Reports are available for download from CFR's website, www.cfr.org.
For more information, email publications@cfr.org.

Made in the USA
Middletown, DE
17 September 2015